Investing for beginners
A Short Read On The Basics Of Investing

Introduction

I want to thank you and congratulate you for downloading the book, "*Investing For Beginners*".

This book has actionable information on how to invest in different avenues to increase wealth.

Investing is the #1 ticket to financial freedom. You perhaps understand one very important thing; being liquid does not equate to being wealthy. If you cannot put your money to good use to work for you, your chances of retiring poor are very high.

The rich men and women of this world started somewhere. Even if we overlook the rich folks born affluent – their forbearers and those before them likely had to start small before they built the family empire. Starting small and making smart investment choices is the path that most now affluent people took to raise their net worth.

If you want to learn how to invest, this book is the ultimate beginner investor guide. It does not matter how old you are: as long as you are willing to follow the contents discussed in this book, you will undoubtedly grow your wealth and get a little closer to financial freedom i.e. a place where you can enjoy the freedom of not having to work for money to make ends meet. The idea is to be smart and as you know, you cannot be smart without knowing i.e. without having the necessary information.

If you are looking for comprehensive information to get you started in the journey to building an empire, this book is what you need along the way. You will discover the different avenues you can invest in, how to deal with risk and much more to ensure your journey to building wealth is seamless.

Thanks again for downloading this book. I hope you enjoy it!

© **Copyright 2017 by Daniel D'apollonio - All rights reserved.**

This document is geared towards providing exact and reliable information in regards to the topic and issue covered. The publication is sold with the idea that the publisher is not required to render accounting, officially permitted, or otherwise, qualified services. If advice is necessary, legal or professional, a practiced individual in the profession should be ordered.

- From a Declaration of Principles which was accepted and approved equally by a Committee of the American Bar Association and a Committee of Publishers and Associations.

In no way is it legal to reproduce, duplicate, or transmit any part of this document in either electronic means or in printed format. Recording of this publication is strictly prohibited and any storage of this document is not allowed unless with written permission from the publisher. All rights reserved.

The information provided herein is stated to be truthful and consistent, in that any liability, in terms of inattention or otherwise, by any usage or abuse of any policies, processes, or directions contained within is the solitary and utter responsibility of the recipient reader. Under no circumstances will any legal responsibility or blame be held against the publisher for any reparation, damages, or monetary loss due to the information herein, either directly or indirectly.

Respective authors own all copyrights not held by the publisher.

The information herein is offered for informational purposes solely, and is universal as so. The presentation of the information is without contract or any type of guarantee assurance.

The trademarks that are used are without any consent, and the publication of the trademark is without permission or backing by the trademark owner. All trademarks and brands within this book are for clarifying purposes only and are the owned by the owners themselves, not affiliated with this document.

Table of Contents

Introduction

Chapter 1: How to Invest Your First $ 1000

- 1: Investing in Mutual Funds and Exchange-Traded Funds
- 2: Investing In Certificates Of Deposit
- Nuggets of Wisdom to Adopt As You Invest Your First $1,000

Chapter 2: Stock Investing For Beginners

- Four Major Ways in Which You Can Invest Your Money in Stocks
- The Five Types of Assets You Might Own When You Invest
- The 3 Financial Statements Necessary for Stock Investing

Chapter 3: Real Estate Investing for Beginners – What You Need to Know in the Novice Stage

- What Is Real Estate Investing?
- Real Estate Investing Through REITs

Chapter 4: A Beginners Step-by-Step Overview of Dividends & How they Work

- How Companies Pay Dividends

Chapter 5: The Concept of Compounding & 5 Investment Tips for the Beginner

Conclusion

If you are completely new to investing, perhaps you might be wondering; where can you invest the extra cash you have so that it can work for you without putting it at risk, of course. In the first chapter, we will be discussing how to put your first $1000 to work for you!

Chapter 1: How to Invest Your First $ 1000

After scraping up some money on the side, money that you can comfortably use without having worrying about repaying a pending debt or the health of your emergency fund, you are in a position where you can invest.

If you are in this position (and it makes sense to think you are indeed there given that you are reading this book), you should try investing.

While a mere pittance to seasoned investors, $1,000 is a decent enough amount for many of us. This section of the guide will not suggest what you should invest in, No; we shall instead look at the suggestions several investment experts give to investment beginners who have a thousand dollars to spare. This section will highlight several investment options that will be "safer" when compared to the others we shall discuss in other sections of this course. However, investing is itself, risk taking. You must also know that this book will not be limited to these options: even as a beginner, you can invest in just about anything provided you go about it with while being very calculative about taking risks.

What Do You Invest Your First 1,000 Dollars In?

Before you consider the investment options detailed in this section, you must remember that investing is a process that takes times. For the beginner, this is certainly the case. It is not in the interests of this book to ward you away from investing. However, if you feel as if you will need that $1,000 in a few months, the best thing you can do is add it to your rainy day fund. The other thing to note is that you must never invest an amount you are not 100% prepared to lose; after all, investing is, primarily, a risk.

Certainly, others will also say that by refusing to invest, you are risking plenty. That stands to reason too. If you have an extra thousand to spare, then consider investing your money into the following options:

1: Investing in Mutual Funds and Exchange-Traded Funds

Mutual funds and exchange-traded funds are usually good products for young folk who do not have ample assets to draw up a diversified portfolio.

A mutual fund is simply "a basket of multiple investments." Investors put any amount of money they want into the basket. The usual mutual fund basket may have $500-million or even $1-billion. Mutual funds have a mutual fund manager who is in charge of making decisions on where to invest the basket of money.

An ETF is quite similar to a mutual fund except many of them do not have a manager in the same fashion as mutual funds. Let us say you purchase an ETF that does follow the Toronto Stock Exchange; essentially, you are buying into, via the ETF, all the different stocks Toronto Stock Exchange has. Let me explain:

Exchange-Traded Funds

Exchange-traded funds also go by ETFs. Ever since their introduction into the world some 20 years ago, ETFs have been steadily growing in popularity. Just like stocks, you can buy or sell ETFs on an exchange at any time during a trading day. However, like mutual funds, an ETF will hold a "basket" of assets, with the example of tech stocks, or, in a broader form, the United States stock market.

Jake Loescher has this to say about ETFs, *"They provide broad, asset-class exposure and they will do this for an incredibly cheap cost."* Jake Loescher is not some fancy nobody with an interest in the machinery and cogs of investment. Jake is a financial advisor at Savant Capital Management, a fee-only money management company that has its headquarters in Rockford, Illinois.

While a veteran investor who has bottomless pockets may opt to invest in mutual funds over ETFs, ETFs are accessible to the beginning investor looking to invest his or her money wisely.

Mutual Funds

Do not take the above paragraph as an incentive to give up on mutual funds simply because you are a novice investor. While ETFs are a superior option for the beginner, investing in mutual funds is a great option for you.

Here is what Jake Loescher has to say about mutual funds, "Most of those Vanguard Target Retirement mutual funds are incredibly easy to draw up. This is so even for the unsophisticated investor. They also offer a broad asset-allocation exposure, just like ETFs, at a minimum funding standard of $1,000. They will also offer you automatic rebalancing, as you get closer and closer to retirement."

Supposing you cannot decide whether to invest in ETFs or a mutual funds, what then?
If you are debating whether to invest in a mutual fund or ETF, you have to consider whether the $1,000 you are putting up is a singular investment or merely the beginning of a long-term plan to invest money each month.
If you are in a position where you can afford to put away some cash each month for your retirement, a mutual fund is the better choice. It is an even superior choice if you are contributing this money to a 401(k) plan or an IRA. Both of these come with tax advantages.
David Nawrocki, a finance professor at the prestigious Villanova School of Business in Pennsylvania says, "*A lot of mutual funds come with a $1,000 minimum, with minimum deposits of $25*".

2: Investing In Certificates Of Deposit

Certificates of deposit are among the safest investments options you will ever find anywhere. One reason for this is the fact that the FDIC (Federal Deposit Insurance Corporation) insures them. So technically, the United States insures your money. Since the US is insuring your investment, it is impossible to lose your money in a CD.

This safety does have its own downside. Since there is virtually zero risk, there will not be much in way of interest. Most of the highest yielding, one-year CDs have an interest rate of under one percent (www.bankrate.com). There are banks that will offer zero-penalty CDs. This means if you do need to withdraw your money early, you will not get slapped with a fee as the case would normally be.

Nuggets of Wisdom to Adopt As You Invest Your First $1,000

As you invest your first $1,000, consider the following nuggets of wisdom:

1. Start Conservatively

"*New investors will be wise to begin very conservatively,*" advises Diana Webb, an assistant professor of finance at Northwood University. She continues, "*If you are a new investor and you experience a poor market while you are still in the early beginnings of investing, you will likely be frightened away and afterwards, very wary of the investing world.*"

2. Take Risks

Webb, despite her advice to be conservative, encourages new investors to take risks, especially if they are younger. Here is how to go about it:

The risk taking formula: Ideally, Webb says that you ought to subtract your current age from 100. Thus if you are 25 years old, 75 percent of what you invest can be placed in something that is a bit risky like the stock market. You can then direct the remaining 25% into an investment scheme that is safe/less risky like the U.S. government savings bond or CD.

The current composite rate on such a savings bond is about 1.8 percent. If you are interested, you can buy them from the Treasury (www.treasurydirect.gov).

Let's take the discussion a little further by discussing how to invest in stocks in the next chapter.

Chapter 2: Stock Investing For Beginners

Investing in the stock market is a learned art.
If, like many new investors in the stock market, you are confused on what to do, don't worry; many others started where you are now. How do you go about it? How do you structure your moves so that you make the least number of mistakes as possible? You can stop worrying; this section shall help you invest in stocks. We are going to start by discussing the basics of stock investing before moving on to the more advanced areas in the field.
If you know what to do and actually go ahead and do it, achieving stock investing success is not difficult.
So what are the investment options in stock investing? Here are 4 of them:

Four Major Ways in Which You Can Invest Your Money in Stocks

Typically, you can invest your cash in stocks in four major ways:
1. Investing via a 401k plan – if you happen to work for a non-profit organization, a 403b plan
2. Investing via a traditional IRA, a Roth IRA, a Simple IRA, or a SEP IRA account
3. Investing via brokerage accounts
4. Investing via a straight up stock purchase-plan, or a dividend reinvestment plan (also known as a DRIP)

When you invest in stocks, you are likely to have any of the following 5 types of assets depending on the way in which you invested:

The Five Types of Assets You Might Own When You Invest

Generally, the average investor will likely own five asset types in his ownership lifetime. This is dependent on whether such an investor decides to invest in the assets directly or decides to do it via a pooled structure such as mutual funds, index funds, exchange traded funds, or hedge funds. Here are these five asset types:

1: Common stocks – Every time you invest in a stock, what happens is that you acquire some ownership stake in an operating business. It does not end there – you also own the net earnings of that share and the resulting dividends produced by that firm.

Although you do not have to channel your money into stock investing to get wealthy, you should know that over the last 200 years or so, equities (stocks) have by far been the asset class with the highest returns and along the same lines, have brought forth the most wealth.

2: Preferred stocks – Preferred stocks are unique types of stock that often pay higher dividends but have a limited upside.

3: Bonds – Many new investors have heard of bonds. While some of these investors have an idea of what bonds are, many of them do not really know what bonds are. Let us examine bonds.

When you lend your money to your country, your municipality, your business, or some other institution that qualifies as one, what you do is purchase bonds. Some examples of bonds are the corporate bond, municipal bond, savings bond, U.S. government Treasury bond, etc. These (bonds) pay a certain interest at set terms over a certain period.

4: Money markets – These are highly liquid investments designed in such a way that they protect your buying power. Investors regard them as a cash equivalent. There are 2 varieties of money markets: the money market accounts, and the money market funds.

5: Real estate investment trusts, also known as REITs – This is a special kind of corporation designation that allows for no taxation at the corporate level provided that more than 90 percent of earnings are paid to the shareholders. These assets are usually invested in several real estate projects as well as properties.

So how exactly should you go about investing in stocks? Well, whatever type of assets or types of stocks you invest in, you will need to be careful in your selection process. Let's learn more about that.

The 3 Financial Statements Necessary for Stock Investing

Before you buy ownership stake in a corporation or company by investing in the stock it has to offer, you should closely examine three financial statements. These 3 are:
1. The income statement (profit and loss account)
2. The cash flow statement
3. The balance sheet

You can learn how to interpret financial statements here, here and here.
Note: All of these three financial statements will work together and will reinforce each another. For this reason, you cannot simply isolate them and study them in separate form. If you insist on doing this, you will find yourself making many vital decisions based on little more than partial data: a massive mistake that may well be expensive especially if you decide you want to invest in stocks rather than investing in a more senior security that is higher up in the conventional capital structure. An example of this is a bond.

The Importance of Researching When Investing in Stocks

When you are researching a stock investment, there are typically 5 documents you want to ensure you get your hands on to research a potential stock's relative merit:
1: The Form 10-K – the Form 10-K is the yearly filing with the SEC (Securities and Exchange Commission) and it is probably the most important document of research available to an investor about a firm or company.
2: The Most Recent Form 10-Q – The Form 10-Q is the quarterly version of a company's Form 10-K.
3: Proxy statement – This includes information on the Board of Directors as well as management compensation and shareholder proposals
4: The most recently updated annual report – you ought to read the Chairman's and the CEO's reports and sometimes the CFO's or other officers of high ranking so as to see just how they view that particular business.

Here is the thing you need to know: *not all annual reports are drawn up equally.* The mistake most investors, including some seasoned ones, make is that they think the chairperson's annual report speaks for everyone. A lot of the time, it does not.

5: A statistical showing going back 5 or even 10 years – Some companies like to prepare this kind of information in easy to digest formats. Sure enough, they will mostly do this for a subscription fee.

If you've 'graduated' from stocks and want to take your portfolio a step further, you can move to investing in real estate. Let's discuss the specifics in the next chapter.

Chapter 3: Real Estate Investing for Beginners – What You Need to Know in the Novice Stage

Real estate investing is undoubtedly one of the oldest forms of investing having been alive since back in the early years of settled civilization. Predating the modern stock markets, we can comfortably say that real estate is one of the 5 top asset classes that each investor ought to seriously consider including in an investment portfolio.

Here are advantages to investing in real estate:

- ✓ Unique cash flow
- ✓ Liquidity
- ✓ Profitability
- ✓ Unique net worth characteristics
- ✓ Diversification benefits

In this section on investing in real estate as a new investor, we shall go through some real estate basics and look at the more in-depth areas and the concepts within them so you can learn how to enter into the real estate investment world.

We will start at the beginning; what exactly constitutes real estate investing?

What Is Real Estate Investing?

Real estate investing is a broad class of investing, operating, and financial activity centered on generating income from tangible property or properties, or generating cash flow somehow tied to the said tangible property.
Real estate property ordinarily falls into one of the categories below:

- ✓ Residential real estate
- ✓ Mixed-use real estate
- ✓ Retail real estate
- ✓ Industrial real estate
- ✓ Commercial real estate

With this in mind, it is clear there are a myriad of varied real estate investment types you can consider for your portfolio.

Investing in Real Estate to Generate Rental Income

To understand real estate investing for generating rental income purposes, we need to demystify the concept of rental real estate:
In its purest, most basic form, the central concept behind investing in real estate is that you, the investor, (also the landlord) acquires some tangible property; it could be raw, sprawling farmland, some land with a cottage built on it, some land that has an office building, land that has an industrial warehouse on it, or just about anything.

You then go out and find a person who is interested in using this property. This person/entity is whom we call a tenant. You and the tenant proceed to enter into an agreement that binds both parties. You will grant the tenant access to your real estate property so that he/she can use it under terms of your making for a specified time length and with a few restrictions.

Some of these restrictions are not your idea; they are the federal, state, and local law. Others you agree upon in what we refer to as the lease contract or the rental agreement. In exchange, your tenant will pay you for putting your real estate to personal use. The payment you expect from this is what we call "rent."

It is thus no surprise that for many investors, this has a major psychological benefit over say, investing in a stock or a bonds. As such an investor, you can take a drive to the property, you can see it, get to touch it with your hands, and even drive laps around it if you fancy.

You can grab a can of paint and proceed to paint it your favorite color. You can hire some architect or even a construction company to do some modifications to it. Moreover, you can use your negotiation skill to settle on a viable rental rate.

The Capitalization Rate Conundrum

Capitalization rate, also referred to as the cap rate, refers to the ratio of (NOI) Net Operating Income to property asset value. Therefore, for example, if a $2million property generates a NOI of $200,000, its cap rate would be 10% i.e. $200,000: 2,000,000.

From time to time, a lot of real estate investors become as misguided and misinformed as a lot of stock investors become when stock market bubbles crop up. They insist that cap rates do not matter. They are wrong! Do not fall for this nonsense whenever you come across it (and you will).

If you price rental rates properly and appropriately, you will enjoy proper rate of return on capital after you have accounted for such factors as property cost, which includes depreciation reserves, property and income tax, insurance, maintenance, as well as other relative expenditures. Additionally, you must measure the amount of time you require to deal with your investment because your time is hands down the most valuable asset you have. Why do you think a passive income is that valuable to investors if not for the time factor? Once you determine your holdings to be large enough, you may then establish or even hire a property management company that will take care of the daily operations of your portfolio. The company will do this in exchange for some percentage of your rental revenue.

Real Estate Investing Through REITs

One way you can invest in real estate in a format that is a bit similar to how you invest in stocks is buying real estate investment trusts, also known as REITs. You can do this via a brokerage account, a Roth IRA, or any other custody account.

REITs are unique in that the tax structure they are under came into being way back when the Eisenhower administration was working hard to encourage smaller investors to invest in those real estate projects they otherwise could not afford. Examples of such were shopping centers and hotels.

Corporations that opt for the REIT treatment do not pay Federal income tax on corporate earnings so long as they conform to a few rules. One of these rules is to distribute 90 percent or more of their profits to the shareholders in dividend form.

One downside to investing in REITs is that unlike the common stock, the dividends paid out are not "qualified dividends." This means the owner cannot take advantage of low tax rates available for the bulk of dividends. Instead, the taxation for dividends from your real estate investment trusts will be at your personal rate. On the upside, IRS has ruled that REIT dividends, which are usually generated within tax shelters such as a Rollover IRA will largely not be subject to unrelated business income tax. With this in mind, you may be able to keep them in a retirement account without worrying about tax complexity.

Whether you are investing in real estate or stocks, some forms of these investment yield returns in the form of dividends. In the next chapter, we will learn about dividends.

Chapter 4: A Beginners Step-by-Step Overview of Dividends & How they Work

Here is how dividends work:

How Companies Pay Dividends

Companies that earn profits may opt to do either of the following: *pay the profit out to shareholders, reinvest the profit in the company via expansion, channeling them toward debt reduction, or repurchasing shares, or perform both actions.*

When a company pays out a profit portion to the company's shareholders, this payment is what we call a dividend. For most investors, the action of "living off dividends" is the ultimate goal.

During the 1st part of the 20th century, dividends were the sole reason investors bothered to purchase stock. In fact, Wall Street fellows loved to say, *"The only use of a company is to pay out dividends."* Today, there is no doubt that the investor's view is a lot more refined.

The Process

As far as dividends go, there is a process. Dividends should be declared (i.e. approved) by the company's Board of Directors every time they are paid out. In regards to a company's dividends, there are three vital dates to remember.

1. Declaration date: The date of declaration, which is the day the Board of Directors announces their intention to pay out dividends. On this particular day, the company will create a liability for themselves: the company now owes its stockholders money. On this date, the company's Board will make sure to announce record as well as a payment date.

2. Date of record: This one is also called the "ex-dividend" date. It is the day the stockholder of record is entitled to his upcoming dividend payout. According to Barron's, the stock will typically start trading ex-dividend on the fourth business day before payment date. To put it plainly, only the shareowners before or on that date will get to receive dividends. If you bought shares of Prime Yoghurt after their ex-dividend date, you would not expect to receive the upcoming dividend payment that investors from whose shares you purchased would.

3. Payment date: This is everyone's favorite date. On this date, the company actually pays out dividends to its shareholders. Here is something else you need to know: *most companies pay the bulk of dividends 4 times per year (on a quarterly basis).* This means that when you as an investor see that the Coca-Cola Company is paying a $0.88 dividend, you will be receiving $0.22 for every share 4 times a year.

About Cash Dividends, Property Dividends, and Unique One Time Dividends

Cash Dividends: Regular cash dividends are the dividends paid out of the company's profits to the owner of that business (this means the shareholders). A business that has preferred stock issued should pay the dividends on those shares before directing a dime in the way of the common stockholder.

Property Dividends: A property dividend is the dividend paid out when a company opts to distribute property to its shareholders rather than paying out in the form of cash or stocks. Property dividends may take the form of such things as cocoa beans, railroad cars, gold, pencils, salad dressing silver, or any other "property", which has a tangible value. Such dividends are usually recorded at market value on the date of declaration.

Special/Unique One-Time Dividends: There are times a company will actually pay a special one-time dividend in addition to paying out the regular dividend. Well, the truth is that these are rare and normally occur for several reasons such as a major litigation win, liquidation of a certain investment, or the successful sale of a business. They may be in the form of stock cash, or even property dividends.

To add on, there are times when these dividends may be categorized as a "capital return." This means these payments are not payouts of the firm's profits but are instead a return of the money shareholders have invested in it. The result is that return of these capital dividends is tax free.

Next, we will learn about stock splits as well as how they differ from stock dividends.

Stock Dividends and How They Differ From Stock Splits

Here is how stock dividends differ from stock splits:

Stock Dividends: A stock dividend is a distribution of extra shares of the company's stock to the owners of common stock. A company might opt to pay out stock dividends for any number of reasons such as the desire to lower stock price on a per share basis in a bid to prompt an increase in trading as well as increase liquidity or an inadequate amount of cash at hand.

Why does lowering stock-price increase liquidity? Overall, folks will be more likely to purchase and then sell a $50 stock than they are a $5,000 stock. The result is a large number of the company's shares trading hands every day.

Here is an example to help you understand this better:

Company X has a million shares of regular stock. This company has a total of 5 investors, each of whom owns 200,000 shares. This stock is currently trading at $100 a share, thus giving this business a market cap of $100 million.

The management then decides to issue a 20 percent stock dividend. It goes on to print up an extra 200,000 shares of regular stock (basically, 20% of a million) and then sends these to its shareholders based on the current ownership. Each of these investors owns 200,000 shares or a fifth of this company so they each get 40,000 of these new shares (a fifth of the 200,000 new shares issued).

Now, our company has 1.2 million shares that are outstanding; every investor now owns 240,000 shares of regular stock. The 20% dilution in the value of every share, however, makes the stock price fall to $83.33. Here is the vital bit: our company (as well as our investors) is still in the very same position it was in. Instead of every investor owning 200,000 shares each at $100, they now have 240,000 shares each going at $83.33 or business' market cap is still at a flat $100 million.

Next, we will cover one of the most important concepts of investing i.e. compounding.

Chapter 5: The Concept of Compounding & 5 Investment Tips for the Beginner

You have some money – perhaps not a lot of it, but you have some to spare – and it is your intention to see it multiply like rice in a pot.

Once you have the essentials (savings, budgeting, and debt) sorted, you should consider investing the money you have. Many people feel overwhelmed when starting out in investing. It is likely they feel as if they do not belong, which is a wrong way of thought. Of course you belong, you are human, are you not?

In addition to the rest of the material in this book, here are some investment tips to help you out:

1: Start Right Now

You are never too green or too young to begin putting away small amounts monthly. Whether you are working a steady job or not, if you can manage to spare some bucks, do it. The other thing to understand is that no amount is too small to save and invest. If $25 is all you can afford to put away every month, go ahead and put it away.

Here is some common sense knowledge for you: the longer you invest, the more money you stand to make; of course, you are going to have ups and downs. However, if you invest from age 23 versus someone who begins at age 33, and you both invest until you are 53 years old, you will end up with more money not just because you have been going at it longer, but also because of compounding rates of return.

2: Speak To People Who Have the Knowledge

Few things are as potent as proper knowledge. Therefore, find out what your options are. Speak to the friendly investment advisor at your local bank about whether or not you ought to open up a tax-free savings account (also known as a TFSA) or invest your money in your retirement savings plan.
Once you comprehend the different account types, the benefits, and lows, you are more educated and thus able to make informed decisions.

3: Start With What Is Familiar

An incredibly easy way to get into the stock market, for instance, is by purchasing things you are familiar with and understand. If you like to drink your green tea latte every day, why not buy Starbucks shares. However, you have to separate this from serious investing.

We are not saying that investing in companies whose product you are familiar with is not on the serious side of investing. However, this is a strategy best employed when you are starting out and are still young in the field. As you spend more time and money in the investing world, it is best to extrapolate some of Apostle Paul's teachings in your dabbling –*"when I was a child, I did as children did. When I became a man, I ceased my childish ways."* 1 Corinthians 13:11

4: Diversify

It is a little foolish to have all your money in one investment vehicle; after all, investing is a risk. To be safe, you need to spread out your money over several investments. What is more, you stand to enjoy different interest rates for your investments when you diversify, which is a good thing.

5: DIY

Your local bank might have a discount broker's arm. Why not open up an account and trade yourself? However, you should know that if you do go through a discount broker, no one will give you directives on what to purchase, when to purchase it, or when to make a sale. You will have to perform your own research and figure this stuff out yourself.

Conclusion

Investing, while not easy or straightforward, is not as daunting as many make it to be. All it takes is actively seeking knowledge and using your wits. You also need to understand that failure is always possible and if you stay in the game long enough, you will have to take the good with the bad a lot of the time. Even as others reward you greatly, some investments will burn you. Investing is a fluid world. Despite that, understand that you belong: It is your world too, if you will allow it to be.

Thank you again for downloading this book!
I hope this book was able to help you to understand how to build wealth through investing.
The next step is to implement what you have learnt.

Finally, if you enjoyed this book, would you be kind enough to leave a review for this book on Amazon?

Click here to leave a review for this book on Amazon!

Thank you and good luck!

www.ingramcontent.com/pod-product-compliance
Lightning Source LLC
Chambersburg PA
CBHW061239180526
45170CB00003B/1363